# Goat Milk Soap Making

## Handmade Goat Milk Soap Recipes for Clean and Healthy Skin and Energy Boosting

Natural Goat Milk Soaps

Book 5

Janela Maccsone

**ISBN:** 9798545112395

# Natural and Homemade Soaps

Have you ever dreamed of making natural goat milk soap by yourself? If earlier one could only dream about homemade soap, today it has become a reality.

Homemade goat milk soap is always an exclusive product. Making handmade soap is a fun and completely uncomplicated process!

It is a great idea for a small home business. If you want to start your own business, but are still new to entrepreneurship, then think about this idea. The production of homemade soap does not require specific knowledge or big investments; everyone can master the technology of soap making.

You do not need to purchase complex tools. All you need is creativeness. The popularity of handmade soap is growing due to the exclusivity. Everything is based on the ability to prepare natural and fragrant soap.

# Chapter 1: Cold Process Goat Milk Soaps

## Cherry and Coconut Goat Milk Soap

**Prep Time: about 45 minutes**

**Ingredients:**

- 16 oz cherry essential oil
- 16 oz coconut butter
- 12 oz coconut oil
- 8 oz palm oil
- 5 oz castor oil
- 8 oz soap base
- 5 oz goat milk

**How to Make Homemade Soap:**

**1.** Chop the soap base.

**2.** Melt the soap base pieces over the low heat for 20 minutes and then cool the melted soap base. Pour the goat milk and mix well until there is a smooth mass.

**3.** Melt the coconut butter, coconut oil, palm oil and castor oil over the low heat for 20 minutes. Cool the oils and stir well.

**4.** Mix together the oils with the soap base and milk. Next melt for 5-10 minutes. Add in the cherry essential oil and blend using a stick blender until there is a homogenous mass.

**5.** Pour the mixture into the molds.

**6.** After 20-24 hours remove the soap from the molds and cut it. Now you are free to use the soap.

# Goat Milk, Coconut and Cinnamon Soap

**Prep Time: 40-50 minutes**

**Ingredients:**

- 10 oz coconut essential oil
- 2 oz coconut butter
- 10 oz palm oil
- 8 oz castor oil
- 8 oz cinnamon essential oil
- 6 oz soap base
- 6 oz goat milk

**How to Make Homemade Soap:**

**1.** Pour the goat milk into the soap base and melt the soap base pieces in a water bath for about 20 minutes.

**2.** In the microwave, melt the coconut butter, palm oil and castor oil for 10 minutes.

**3.** Combine the oils mix with the soap base. Add in the cinnamon essential oil and coconut essential oil. Melt the mixture over the low heat for 10 minutes and stir well.

**4.** Pour the mixture into the molds and cool.

**5.** Remove the soap from the molds and cut it into pieces. Use the soap.

# Goat Milk, Coconut and Lemon Soap

**Prep Time: about 50 minutes**

## Ingredients:

- 10 oz coconut essential oil
- 5 oz lemon zest, minced
- 14 oz olive oil
- 12 oz palm oil
- 10 oz castor oil
- 2 tablespoons shredded coconut
- 8 oz coconut butter
- 10 oz goat milk
- 8 oz lye

## How to Make Homemade Soap:

**1.** Pour the goat milk into the bowl and keep it in the refrigerator for about few hours.

**2.** Next, pour the lye into the cold goat milk and mix well until there is a smooth consistency. Use the rubber gloves and goggles. Leave the lye and goat milk mixture in the well ventilated place.

**3.** Then mix together the coconut butter with the oils and melt for 20 minutes. Keep stirring to prevent the butter and oils from rising and burning.

**4.** Pour the lye and goat milk mixture into the oils and mix well. Spoon the lemon zest.

**5.** Spoon the shredded coconut and blend the mixture well using a stick blender or food processor until there is a smooth and homogenous consistency.

**6.** Spoon the soap batter into the square molds. In a few days take the soap out of the molds and cut it into pieces. Wait for few weeks until the process of the saponification will complete and only then use the soap.

During the soap preparation process always use rubber gloves, goggles, long sleeves and breathing mask.

# Goat Milk, Coconut and Pear Soap

**Prep Time: about 20-30 minutes**

**<u>Ingredients:</u>**

- 4 tablespoons coconut essential oil
- 4 tablespoons pear fragrance oil
- 15 oz olive oil
- 10 oz coconut butter
- 12 oz palm oil
- 5 oz 100% pure lye
- 8 oz goat milk

**<u>How to Make Homemade Soap:</u>**

**1.** Slowly poon the lye into the cold goat milk and mix well until the lye dissolves. The fumes will be produced during the lye melting process, so remember to wear the rubber gloves, goggles and breathing mask.

**2.** Cool the lye mixture for about few hours until the inner temperature reaches 85-95 degrees Fahrenheit. Place the mixture into the ventilated room.

**3.** Combine the olive and palm oils.

**4.** Heat the coconut butter for around 10 minutes stirring all the time to prevent the butter from burning.

**5.** Add in the oils and stir well. Spoon the pear fragrance oil and coconut essential oil.

**6.** Then pour the lye and goat milk mixture into the pot with the oils and blend the mixture well using a stick blender.

**7.** Pour the mixture into the molds. In a few days take the soap out of the molds and set aside for a few weeks. Remember to wait until the process of the saponification will complete and then use the soap.

During the soap preparation process always use rubber gloves, goggles, long sleeves and breathing mask.

# Goat Milk, Cherry and Peppermint Soap

**Prep Time: about 30-40 minutes**

**Ingredients:**

- 10 oz cherry essential oil
- 10 oz peppermint essential oil
- 2 oz lemon essential oil
- 1 tablespoon beeswax
- 15 oz palm oil
- 8 oz castor oil
- 6 oz olive oil
- 6 oz shea butter
- 7 oz lye
- 8 oz goat milk

## How to Make Homemade Soap:

**1.** Spoon the lye into the cold goat milk and mix well until there is a smooth consistency and creamy mass. Wear the rubber gloves, goggles and long sleeves.

**2.** Set the lye and goat milk batter aside to cool. Place the heat resistant container or pot with the lye/milk batter into the sink with the cold water.

**3.** Melt the palm, castor and olive oils with the shea butter over the low heat for 20 minutes.

**4.** Then spoon the lye mixture into the oils.

**5.** Pour the cherry essential oil, lemon essential oil, peppermint essential oil and beeswax.

**6.** Blend the ingredients well using a stick blender until there is a smooth and creamy mass.

**7.** Pour the mixture into the molds. In 4-5 days take the soap out of the molds and cut it into pieces. Then set the soap aside for few weeks until the process of saponification will complete and only then use the soap.

During the soap preparation process always use rubber gloves, goggles, long sleeves and breathing mask.

# Cold Process Goat Milk, Strawberry and Honey Soap

**Prep Time: about 40-60 minutes**

## Ingredients:

- 10 oz strawberry essential oil
- 4 tablespoons liquid honey
- 2 tablespoons honey fragrance oil
- 14 oz palm oil
- 8 oz castor oil
- 10 oz shea butter
- 8-9 oz goat milk
- 8 oz lye

## How to Make Homemade Soap:

**1.** Slowly pour the pure lye into the cold goat milk and mix well until there is a homogenous mass.

**2.** Set the pot with the lye and goat milk aside. Let it cool for around half an hour until the inner temperature reaches 80-90 degrees Fahrenheit. Place the mixture into the well-ventilated room.

**3.** In the pot, combine the palm oil and castor oil and melt the oils on a burner over the low heat for 10 minutes. Keep stirring the oils while heating to prevent the oils from burning.

**4.** Add the shea butter into the oils and melt them over the low heat for around 10 minutes.

**5.** When the lye and oils have the same temperature, slowly spoon the lye mixture into the oils. Stir for 5 minutes and then use a stick blender to blend until there is a smooth consistency.

**6.** Mix in the strawberry essential oil, honey fragrance oil and liquid honey.

**7.** Stir well and pour the mixture into the molds and set the soap aside. The soap should harden, so keep it in molds for at least few days. Then cut the soap into smaller bars and after the two weeks use the soap.

**During the soap preparation process always use rubber gloves, goggles, long sleeves and breathing mask.**

# Goat Milk, Raspberry and Pear Soap

**Prep Time: approximately 30-40 minutes**

**Ingredients:**

- 10 oz raspberry fragrance oil
- 10 oz pear fragrance oil
- 15 oz olive oil
- 13 oz palm oil
- 7 oz castor oil
- 10 oz shea butter
- 10 oz goat milk
- 8 oz lye

## How to Make Homemade Soap:

**1.** Spoon the pure lye into the cold goat milk and mix well until there is a smooth consistency. Keep stirring since the goat milk should remain cold. Remember that the fumes will be produced during this process, so wear the rubber gloves, goggles and breathing mask.

**2.** Cool the lye and goat milk batter until the temperature reaches 80-90 degrees Fahrenheit. Place the mixture in the well-ventilated room or on the balcony.

**3.** Combine the olive, palm and castor oils with the shea butter and melt the oils on a burner over the low heat for about 20 minutes. Keep stirring the oils while heating to prevent them from overheating.

**4.** Slowly spoon the lye mixture into the oils. Blend using a stick blender to blend until there is a smooth consistency and creamy mass.

**5.** Mix in the pear fragrance oil and raspberry fragrance oil.

**6.** Stir well and pour the mixture into the molds.

**7.** The soap should harden, so keep it in molds for at least few days. Cut the soap into bars and place in the ventilated room for two or three weeks and then use the soap.

During the soap preparation process always use rubber gloves, goggles, long sleeves and breathing mask.

# Goat Milk, Strawberry-Lemon Soap

**Prep Time: about 30 minutes**

## Ingredients:

- 8 oz strawberry fragrance oil
- 3 teaspoons folded lemon essential oil
- 14 oz olive oil
- 6 oz shea butter
- 12 oz palm oil
- 5 oz castor oil
- 8 oz 100% pure lye
- 8 oz goat milk

## How to Make Homemade Soap:

**1.** Spoon the lye into the goat milk and mix well until the lye dissolves. The fumes will be produced during the lye melting process, so remember to wear the rubber gloves, goggles and breathing mask.

**2.** Cool the lye mixture for about half an hour until the inner temperature reaches 85-95 degrees Fahrenheit.

**3.** Mix together the olive, castor and palm oils.

**4.** In a pot, melt the shea butter for around 10 minutes stirring all the time to prevent the butter from burning.

**5.** Add in the oils and mix. Spoon the folded lemon essential oil and strawberry fragrance oil. Blend the mixture until there is a creamy and homogenous mass.

**6.** Then pour the lye and goat milk batter into the pot with the oils and blend the mixture well using a stick blender.

**7.** Pour the mixture into the molds. In a few days take the soap out of the molds and cut it. Remember to wait until the process of the saponification will complete and only then use the soap.

During the soap preparation process always use rubber gloves, goggles, long sleeves and breathing mask.

# Goat Milk, Raspberry and Rose Soap

**Prep Time: 50-60 minutes**

## Ingredients:

- 8 oz raspberry essential oil
- 4 tablespoons rose essential oil
- 4 drops pink soap colorant
- 20 oz palm oil
- 15 oz canola oil
- 5 oz castor oil
- 5 oz shea butter
- 8 oz 100% pure lye
- 9 oz cold goat milk

## How to Make Homemade Soap:

**1.** Spoon the lye into the goat milk and mix well until the creamy and smooth mass. Wear the rubber gloves, goggles and breathing mask, because the fumes will be produced.

**2.** Cool the lye for around 30 minutes until the inner temperature of the mixture reaches 85-95 degrees Fahrenheit. Place the mixture in the ventilated room to cool for 20-30 minutes.

**3.** Mix together the palm, canola and castor oils. Then spoon the the shea butter and melt them over the low heat for 20 minutes or longer until there is a creamy consistency and smooth mass. Set the oils aside and cool the oils for 20 minutes.

**4.** Spoon the lye mixture into the pot with the oils. Mix well until there is a smooth mass.

**5.** Add in the raspberry essential oil, rose essential oil and pink soap colorant and blend the mixture well using a stick blender.

**6.** Spoon the mixture into the molds. In 4-5 days take the soap out of the molds and cut it into pieces. Next, set aside for around two or three weeks and then use the soap.

During the soap preparation process always use rubber gloves, goggles, long sleeves and breathing mask.

# Goat Milk, Strawberry and Cherry Soap

**Prep Time: 50-60 minutes**

## Ingredients:

- 10 oz strawberry essential oil
- 10 oz cherry kernel oil
- 4 drops pink soap colorant
- 23 oz palm oil
- 22 oz canola oil
- 15 oz castor oil
- 10 oz olive oil
- 7 oz coconut butter
- 5 oz shea butter
- 8 oz 100% pure lye
- 10 oz goat milk

## How to Make Homemade Soap:

**1.** Spoon the lye into the cold goat milk and stir well. Wear the rubber gloves, goggles and breathing mask, because the fumes will be produced.

**2.** Cool the lye and goat milk for around 30 minutes until the inner temperature of the mixture reaches 85-95 degrees Fahrenheit. Place the mixture in the ventilated room to cool for 20-30 minutes.

**3.** Mix together the palm oil, canola oil, castor oil and olive oil. Melt them over the low heat for around 10 minutes. Add the coconut butter and shea butter. Melt them for 10 minutes.

**4.** Ladle the lye mixture into the pot with the oils. Mix well until there is a pureed and creamy mass.

**5.** Mix in the cherry kernel oil, strawberry essential oil and pink soap colorant and stir.

**6.** Pour the mixture into the molds. After 4 days take the soap out of the molds and set aside for around two or three weeks.

During the soap preparation process always use rubber gloves, goggles, long sleeves and breathing mask.

# Goat Milk, Raspberry and Pineapple Soap for Clean Skin

**Prep Time: 60-65 minutes**

**Ingredients:**

- 10 oz raspberry essential oil
- 4 tablespoons pineapple powder
- 4 oz beeswax
- 11 oz palm oil
- 10 oz olive oil
- 8 castor oil
- 15 oz lard
- 3 tablespoons peppermint essential oil
- 8 oz lye
- 10 oz goat milk

## How to Make Homemade Soap:

**1.** Spoon the lye into the cold goat milk and mix well until there is a creamy consistency. Remember that the fumes will be produced during this process, so wear the rubber gloves, goggles and breathing mask.

**2.** Cool the lye mixture until the temperature reaches 90-95 degrees Fahrenheit. Place the stainless steel bowl with the lye and goat milk mixture into the sink filled with the ice cubes and freezing water.

**3.** In the pot, melt the oils (except the peppermint essential oil and raspberry essential oil) and lard over the low heat for around 20 minutes. Cool for about 30 minutes.

**4.** Next carefully spoon the lye into the oils.

**5.** Mix in the raspberry essential oil and peppermint essential oil. Then spoon the beeswax and pineapple powder and mix well.

**6.** Blend the oils and lye/goat milk batter using a stick blender until there is a creamy consistency.

**7.** Pour the mixture into the molds. In 3-4 days take the soap out of the molds and cut it into pieces. Then set the soap aside for around 2 weeks. Remember to wait until the process of the saponification will complete and only then use the soap.

**During the soap preparation process always use rubber gloves, goggles, long sleeves and breathing mask.**

# Goat Milk, Almond and Pear Soap

**Prep Time: about 30-40 minutes**

## Ingredients:

- 10 oz almond fragrance oil
- 10 oz pear fragrance oil
- 15 oz olive oil
- 13 oz palm oil
- 10 oz castor oil
- 8 oz shea butter
- 10 oz goat milk
- 8 oz lye

## How to Make Homemade Soap:

**1.** Add the lye to the goat milk and mix well until there is a creamy mass. Keep stirring since the milk should remain cold. Remember that the fumes will be produced during this process, so wear the rubber gloves, goggles and breathing mask.

**2.** Cool the lye and goat milk mixture for around 60 minutes or longer until the temperature reaches 80-90 degrees Fahrenheit. Place the mixture in the well-ventilated room.

**3.** Mix together the olive, palm and castor oils with the shea butter and melt the oils on a burner over the low heat for about 20 minutes. Keep stirring the oils while heating to prevent them from overheating.

**4.** Mix in the pear fragrance oil and almond fragrance oil.

**5.** Slowly spoon the lye mixture into the oils.

**6.** Blend using a stick blender. Blend the mixture well until there is a smooth mass.

**7.** The soap should harden, so keep it in molds for at least 4 days. Cut the soap into pieces and place in the ventilated room for two or three weeks and then use the soap.

During the soap preparation process always use rubber gloves, goggles, long sleeves and breathing mask.

# Goat Milk, Almond and Orange Soap

**Prep Time: about 30-40 minutes**

## Ingredients:

- 10 oz almond fragrance oil
- 10 oz orange fragrance oil
- 16 oz olive oil
- 15 oz palm oil
- 10 oz castor oil
- 10 oz shea butter
- 10 oz goat milk
- 8 oz lye

## How to Make Homemade Soap:

**1.** Add the lye to the cold goat milk and mix well until there is a smooth mass. Keep stirring since the goat milk should remain cold. Remember that the fumes will be produced during this process, so wear the rubber gloves, goggles and breathing mask.

**2.** Cool the lye and goat milk mixture for around 60 minutes or longer until the temperature reaches 80-90 degrees Fahrenheit. Place the mixture in the well-ventilated room.

**3.** Mix together the olive, palm and castor oils with the shea butter and melt the oils on a burner over the low heat for about 20 minutes.

**4.** Mix in the orange fragrance oil and almond fragrance oil.

**5.** Slowly spoon the lye mixture into the oils.

**6.** Blend the mixture well until there is a smooth and homogenous consistency.

**7.** Leave the soap for 5 days. Then take it from out of the molds and cut. Place the soap into the ventilated room for two or three weeks and then use the soap.

During the soap preparation process always use rubber gloves, goggles, long sleeves and breathing mask.

# Goat Milk, Almond, Orange and Grapefruit Soap with Honey

**Prep Time: 60-70 minutes**

## Ingredients:

- 10 oz almond fragrance oil
- 10 oz orange essential oil
- 10 oz grapefruit essential oil
- 2 tablespoons liquid honey
- 2 teaspoons ground barley
- 16 oz olive oil
- 16 oz coconut oil
- 15 oz palm oil
- 12 oz goat milk
- 9-10 oz 100% pure lye

## How to Make Homemade Soap:

**1.** Mix together the olive, coconut and palm oils and stir well. Then pour the oils into a pot and melt them on a burner for 10 minutes. Cool them until the temperature reaches around 80-85 degrees Fahrenheit.

**2.** Then pour the almond, grapefruit and raspberry oils and mix well.

**3.** Spoon the lye into the goat milk and mix well until there is a smooth mass.

**4.** Cool the lye mixture until the temperature reaches about 80-90 degrees Fahrenheit. Leave the mixture in the well-ventilated room or on the balcony.

**5.** Then pour the lye mixture into the pot with the oils.

**6.** Spoon the ground barley and liquid honey. Mix all the ingredients using a stick blender until there is a creamy mass and homogenous consistency.

**7.** Ladle the mixture into the molds. In 4-5 days take the soap out of the molds and cut it. Set the soap aside for at least two weeks.

**During the soap preparation process always use rubber gloves, goggles, long sleeves and breathing mask.**

# Goat Milk, Almond, Banana and Yogurt Soap

**Prep Time: about 40-50 minutes**

**Ingredients:**

- 2 cups of yogurt
- 7 tablespoons almond fragrance oil
- 2 bananas, mashed
- 16 oz olive oil
- 16 oz palm oil
- 14 oz castor oil
- 8 oz pure lye
- 10 oz goat milk

**How to Make Homemade Soap:**

**1.** Cut the bananas into pieces. Then blend them using the stick blender until there is a pureed mass.

**2.** Pour the yogurt into the bowl with the blended bananas and blend the ingredients well using the stick blender until there is a smooth mass.

**3.** Spoon the lye into the cold goat milk and stir well until there is a creamy mass.

**4.** The fumes will be produced during the process. Keep stirring all the time until the lye dissolves completely. Cool the lye until the temperature reaches 85-90 degrees Fahrenheit.

**5.** In the pot, mix together the olive, palm and castor oils and melt them on a burner for about 20 minutes.

**6.** Pour the goat milk and lye mixture into the oils. Stir for 5 minutes and then blend the mixture for 10 minutes until there is a smooth and creamy consistency.

**7.** Then mix in the bananas and yogurt mixture. Spoon the almond fragrance oil. Blend all the ingredients well using a stick blender until you get a pureed mass.

**8.** Then spoon the mixture into the molds. After 20-24 hours take the soap out of the molds and cut into pieces. Wait for few weeks to enable the evaporation of unnecessary liquids and then use the homemade soap.

**During the soap preparation process always use rubber gloves, goggles, long sleeves and breathing mask.**

# Goat Milk, Cherry and Pineapple Soap for Clean Skin

**Prep Time: 60-65 minutes**

## Ingredients:

- 12 oz cherry essential oil
- 4 tablespoons pineapple powder
- 4 oz beeswax
- 12 oz palm oil
- 12 oz olive oil
- 10 castor oil
- 15 oz lard
- 3 tablespoons peppermint essential oil
- 8 oz lye
- 10 oz goat milk

## How to Make Homemade Soap:

**1.** Spoon the lye into the cold goat milk and mix well until there is a creamy mass.

**2.** Cool the lye mixture until the temperature reaches 90-95 degrees Fahrenheit. Place the stainless steel bowl with the lye and goat milk mixture into the sink filled with the ice cubes and freezing water.

**3.** In the pot, melt the oils (except the peppermint essential oil and cherry essential oil) and lard over the low heat for around 20 minutes. Cool for about 30 minutes.

**4.** Next, spoon the lye into the oils.

**5.** Mix in the cherry essential oil and peppermint essential oil. Then spoon the beeswax and pineapple powder and mix well.

**6.** Blend the oils and lye/goat milk batter using a stick blender until there is a creamy consistency.

**7.** Pour the mixture into the molds. In 3-4 days take the soap out of the molds and cut it into pieces. Then set the soap aside for around

2 weeks. Remember to wait until the process of the saponification will complete and only then use the soap.

**During the soap preparation process always use rubber gloves, goggles, long sleeves and breathing mask.**

# Goat Milk, Almond and Cherry Soap

**Prep Time: 30-40 minutes**

## Ingredients:

- 5 tablespoons almond fragrance oil
- 2 tablespoons cherry kernel oil
- 2 teaspoons pink colorant
- 16 oz olive oil
- 13 oz palm oil
- 8 oz castor oil
- 2 teaspoons shea butter
- 10 oz goat milk
- 8 oz 100% pure lye

## How to Make Homemade Soap:

**1.** Spoon the lye into the goat milk and mix well until the lye dissolves completely. The fumes will be produced during this process, so wear the rubber gloves, goggles and breathing mask.

**2.** Set the pot with the lye aside and let it cool for a few hours until the temperature reaches 90-95 degrees Fahrenheit. Place the soap batter into the cool room.

**3.** Melt the shea butter, olive, palm and castor oils in the microwave. Cool the oils until the temperature reaches around 85-95 degrees Fahrenheit.

**4.** Dissolve the pink soap colorant in some water and mix well until the colorant melts.

**5.** Then add in the almond fragrance oil, cherry kernel oil and pink colorant.

**6.** Pour the lye and goat milk mixture into the pot with the oils. Blend all the ingredients until there is a creamy and pureed mass.

**7.** Next, ladle the mixture into the molds. In 4 or 5 days take the soap out of the molds and cut it into pieces. Set the soap aside for few weeks. Wait until the process of the saponification will complete and then use the soap.

During the soap preparation process always use rubber gloves, goggles, long sleeves and breathing mask.

# Goat Milk, Mango and Lemon Soap for Delicate Skin

**Prep Time: 30-40 minutes**

## Ingredients:

- 10 oz mango fragrance oil
- 10 oz lemon essential oil
- 5 oz lemon zest, minced
- 17 oz olive oil
- 15 oz palm oil
- 12 oz castor oil
- 2 teaspoons cocoa butter
- 10 oz goat milk
- 8 oz 100% pure lye

## How to Make Homemade Soap:

**1.** Add the lye to the goat milk and mix well. The fumes will be produced during this process, so wear the rubber gloves, goggles and breathing mask.

**2.** Set the pot with the lye aside and let it cool for a few hours until the temperature reaches 90-95 degrees Fahrenheit. Place the soap batter into the cool room.

**3.** Melt the cocoa butter, olive, palm and castor oils over the low heat for about 10 minutes. Cool the oils until the temperature reaches around 85-95 degrees Fahrenheit.

**4.** Dissolve the pink soap colorant in some goat milk and mix well until the colorant melts.

**5.** Then add in the mango fragrance oil, lemon essential oil and lemon zest.

**6.** Pour the lye and goat milk mixture into the pot with the oils. Blend all the ingredients until there is a creamy and pureed mass.

**7.** Next, ladle the mixture into the molds. In 4 or 5 days take the soap out of the molds and cut it into pieces. Then set the soap aside for two weeks. Wait until the process of the saponification will complete and then use the soap.

**During the soap preparation process always use rubber gloves, goggles, long sleeves and breathing mask.**

# Goat Milk and Apricot Soap with Honey

**Prep Time: 30-40 minutes**

## Ingredients:

- 4 tablespoons apricot kernel oil
- 4 tablespoons liquid honey
- 15 oz olive oil
- 10 oz castor oil
- 10 oz palm oil
- 9 oz goat milk
- 8 oz lye

## How to Make Homemade Soap:

**1.** Spoon the lye into the goat milk and mix well until the lye dissolves completely. Remember that the fumes will be produced during this process, so don't forget to wear the rubber gloves, goggles and breathing mask.

**2.** Cool the lye mixture until the temperature reaches 80-90 degrees Fahrenheit. Leave the lye and goat milk in the well-ventilated room.

**3.** Mix together the olive, castor and palm oils and melt them on a burner for 20 minutes. Set the oils aside to cool until the temperature reaches around 80-90 degrees Fahrenheit.

**4.** Then add in the apricot kernel oil.

**5.** Pour the lye and goat milk mixture into the pot with the oils. Mix well.

**6.** Mix in the liquid honey. Next, blend all the ingredients well using a stick blender until there is a creamy consistency and smooth mass.

**7.** Pour the soap batter into the soap molds. In 4 or 5 days take the soap out of the molds. Set the soap aside for two or three weeks. Remember to wait until the process of the saponification will complete and then use the soap.

During the soap preparation process always use rubber gloves, goggles, long sleeves and breathing mask.

# Goat Milk, Strawberry and Orange Soap for Delicate Skin

**Prep Time: 30-40 minutes**

## Ingredients:

- 10 oz almond oil
- 10 oz strawberry essential oil
- 5 oz orange essential oil
- 2 teaspoons orange zest, minced
- 15 oz olive oil
- 10 oz castor oil
- 8 oz palm oil
- 10 oz cold goat milk
- 8 oz lye

## How to Make Homemade Soap:

**1.** Spoon the lye into the cold goat milk and mix well until the lye dissolves completely. Remember that the fumes will be produced during this process, so don't forget to wear the rubber gloves, goggles and breathing mask.

**2.** Cool the lye mixture until the temperature reaches 80-90 degrees Fahrenheit. Leave the lye and goat milk in the well-ventilated room.

**3.** Mix together the almond, olive, castor and palm oils. Melt the oils and cool them.

**4.** Then add in the strawberry essential oil, orange essential oil and minced orange zest.

**5.** Pour the lye and cold goat milk batter into the pot with the oils. Stir well.

**6.** Blend all the ingredients using a stick blender until there is a creamy mass.

**7.** Transfer the soap batter into the molds. In 4 or 5 days take the soap out of the molds and cut it into pieces. Set the soap aside for two or three weeks. Remember to wait until the process of the saponification will complete and then use the soap.

During the soap preparation process always use rubber gloves, goggles, long sleeves and breathing mask.

# Goat Milk, Apricot and Lemon Soap for Energy Boosting

**Prep Time: 30-40 minutes**

## Ingredients:

- 15 oz apricot essential oil
- 15 oz lemon essential oil
- 2 teaspoons lemon zest, minced
- 2 tablespoons beeswax
- 15 oz olive oil
- 12 oz castor oil
- 10 oz palm oil
- 10 oz goat milk
- 8 oz lye

## How to Make Homemade Soap:

**1.** Spoon the lye into the goat milk and mix well until the lye dissolves completely. Remember that the fumes will be produced during this process, so don't forget to wear the rubber gloves, goggles and breathing mask.

**2.** Cool the lye mixture until the temperature reaches 80-90 degrees Fahrenheit. Leave the lye and goat milk in the well-ventilated room.

**3.** Mix together the olive, castor and palm oils. Then melt the oils on a burner for 10 minutes. Set the oils aside to cool until the temperature reaches around 80-90 degrees Fahrenheit.

**4.** Then spoon the apricot essential oil, lemon essential oil, minced lemon zest and beeswax.

**5.** Pour the lye and milk batter into the pot with the oils.

**6.** Blend all the ingredients well using a stick blender or food processor until there is a homogenous mass.

**7.** Pour the soap batter into the molds. In 4 or 5 days take the soap out of the molds. Set your soap aside for two or three weeks.

Remember to wait until the process of the saponification will complete and then use the soap.

**During the soap preparation process always use rubber gloves, goggles, long sleeves and breathing mask.**

# Goat Milk, Grapefruit and Eucalyptus Soap for Energy Boosting

**Prep Time: about 30-40 minutes**

## Ingredients:

- 15 oz grapefruit essential oil
- 4 teaspoons grapefruit zest, minced
- 4 tablespoons eucalyptus oil
- 3 oz beeswax
- 15 oz palm oil
- 14 oz castor oil
- 12 oz olive oil
- 7 oz lard
- 8 oz 100% pure lye
- 10 oz cold goat milk

## How to Make Homemade Soap:

**1.** Spoon the lye into the cold goat milk and mix well until there is a smooth consistency. The fumes will be produced during this process, so don't forget to wear the rubber gloves, goggles and breathing mask.

**2.** Set the lye and milk aside to cool. Place the heat resistant container or pot with the lye mixture into the sink with the cold water.

**3.** Melt the palm, castor olive oils and lard over the low heat for around 20 minutes. Keep stirring to prevent the oils and lard from burning. Add in the grapefruit zest and cool the oils.

**4.** Next pour the lye mixture into the oils.

**5.** Spoon the grapefruit essential oil and eucalyptus oil. Mix in the beeswax and blend the ingredients using a stick blender until there is a creamy mass.

**6.** Spoon the mixture into the molds. After few days cut the soap. Set the soap aside for few weeks.

During the soap preparation process always use rubber gloves, goggles, long sleeves and breathing mask.

# Goat Milk, Mango and Peppermint Soap for Oily Skin

**Prep Time: about 30-40 minutes**

**<u>Ingredients:</u>**

- 15 oz mango essential oil
- 15 oz peppermint essential oil
- 10 oz beeswax
- 15 oz palm oil
- 12 oz coconut oil
- 10 oz olive oil
- 8 oz shea butter
- 9 oz lye
- 12 oz goat milk

**<u>How to Make Homemade Soap:</u>**

**1.** Spoon the lye into the cold goat milk and mix well until there is a smooth consistency. The fumes will be produced during this process, so don't forget to wear the rubber gloves, goggles and breathing mask.

**2.** Cool the lye batter. Place the heat resistant container or pot with the lye mixture into the sink with the cold water or ice cubes.

**3.** Mix together the palm, coconut and olive oils with the shea butter. Melt the oils mix for 20 minutes.

**4.** Then ladle the lye mixture into the oils.

**5.** Add in the mango essential oil, peppermint essential oil and beeswax and blend the ingredients well using a stick blender until there is a smooth consistency.

**6.** Pour the mixture into the round molds. In 4-5 days take the soap out of the molds and cut it. Then set the soap aside for few weeks. Wait until the process of saponification will complete and only then use the handmade soap.

During the soap preparation process always use rubber gloves, goggles, long sleeves and breathing mask.

# Goat Milk, Grapefruit and Orange Soap for Pimples

**Prep Time: about 20-30 minutes**

**Ingredients:**

- 12 oz grapefruit essential oil
- 10 oz orange essential oil
- 5 oz beeswax
- 14 oz palm oil
- 10 oz castor oil
- 10 oz olive oil
- 8 oz cocoa butter
- 9 oz lye
- 10 oz goat milk

**How to Make Homemade Soap:**

**1.** Spoon the lye into the goat milk and mix well until there is a smooth mass. The fumes will be produced during this process, so don't forget to wear the rubber gloves, goggles and breathing mask.
**2.** Set the lye and goat milk mixture aside to cool. Place the heat resistant container or pot with the lye mixture into the sink with the cold water or ice cubes.
**3.** Combine the palm, castor and olive oils with the cocoa butter. Melt the oils mix for 20 minutes.
**4.** Then ladle the lye mixture into the oils.
**5.** Add the grapefruit essential oil, orange essential oil and beeswax and blend the ingredients well using a stick blender until there is a homogenous and creamy mass.
**6.** Pour the mixture into the acrylic molds. In 4-5 days take the soap out of the molds and cut it. Then set the soap aside for few weeks. Wait until the process of saponification will complete and only then use the homemade soap.

During the soap preparation process always use rubber gloves, goggles, long sleeves and breathing mask.

# Goat Milk, Grapefruit, Lemon and Cheery Soap

**Prep Time: 40-50 minutes**

**Ingredients:**

- 14 oz grapefruit essential oil
- 14 oz lemon essential oil
- 2 tablespoons cherry kernel oil
- 1 tablespoon red colorant
- 15 oz olive oil
- 14 oz palm oil
- 8 oz castor oil
- 2 teaspoons coconut butter
- 10 oz goat milk
- 8 oz lye

## How to Make Homemade Soap:

**1.** Pour the lye into the cold goat milk and mix well. The fumes will be produced during this process, so wear the rubber gloves, goggles and breathing mask.

**2.** Set the pot with the lye aside and let it cool for a few hours until the temperature reaches 90-95 degrees Fahrenheit. Place the soap batter into the cool room.

**3.** Melt the coconut butter, olive, palm and castor oils in the microwave. Cool the oils until the temperature reaches around 80-90 degrees Fahrenheit.

**4.** Dissolve the red soap colorant in some water.

**5.** Next pour the grapefruit essential oil, lemon essential oil, cherry kernel oil and red colorant into the oils mixture and stir well.

**6.** Pour the lye and goat milk into the pot with the oils. Blend all the ingredients well using a stick blender until there is a creamy and smooth consistency.

**7.** Pour the mixture into the molds. In 4-5 days take the soap out of the molds. Set the soap aside for few weeks. Wait until the process of the saponification will complete and then use the soap.

During the soap preparation process always use rubber gloves, goggles, long sleeves and breathing mask.

# Goat Milk, Mango, Banana and Yogurt Soap

**Prep Time: about 40-50 minutes**

**Ingredients:**

- 2 cups of yogurt
- 15 oz mango fragrance oil
- 2 bananas, mashed
- 16 oz olive oil
- 16 oz palm oil
- 16 oz castor oil
- 5 oz shea butter
- 8 oz pure lye
- 10 oz goat milk

## How to Make Homemade Soap:

**1.** Cut the bananas into pieces. Then blend them using the stick blender until there is a creamy mass.

**2.** Pour the yogurt into the bowl with the bananas and blend the ingredients well using the stick blender until there is a creamy and pureed mass.

**3.** Spoon the lye into the cold goat milk and stir well until there is a creamy mass.

**4.** The fumes will be produced during the process. Keep stirring all the time until the lye dissolves completely. Cool the lye until the temperature reaches 85-90 degrees Fahrenheit.

**5.** In the pot, mix together the olive, palm and castor oils and melt them on a burner for about 20 minutes.

**6.** Pour the goat milk and lye mixture into the oils. Stir for 5 minutes and then blend the mixture for 10 minutes until there is a smooth and creamy consistency.

**7.** Then mix in the bananas and yogurt mixture. Pour the almond fragrance oil. Blend all the ingredients well using a stick blender until you get a pureed mass.

**8.** Then spoon the mixture into the molds. After 20-24 hours take the soap out of the molds and cut into pieces. Wait for few weeks to enable the evaporation of unnecessary liquids and then use the homemade soap.

**During the soap preparation process always use rubber gloves, goggles, long sleeves and breathing mask.**

# Chapter 2: Hot Process Goat Milk Soaps

## Goat Milk, Orange and Pear Soap

**Prep Time: about 40-50 minutes**

**Cooking Time: 50 minutes**

**Ingredients:**

- 14 oz orange essential oil
- 10 oz pear fragrance oil
- 16 oz olive oil
- 16 oz palm oil
- 15 oz castor oil
- 8 oz shea butter
- 10-12 oz goat milk
- 9 oz 100% pure lye

**How to Make Homemade Soap:**

**1.** Spoon the lye into the cold goat milk and mix well until there is a homogenous consistency.

**2.** Mix together the olive, palm and castor oils with the shea butter. Melt the oils and shea batter over the low heat for around 20 minutes.

**3.** Put on a mask, rubber gloves and goggles and spoon the lye batter into the oils and stir well.

**4.** Cook the lye and oils mixture over the low heat for about 30 minutes. Keep stirring to prevent the soap batter from burning and rising.

**5.** Use a PH test to check if the soap is ready. Ideal values are between 7 and 10. If the indicator is higher than 10, then this means that the soap is not ready.

**6.** Mix in the orange essential oil and pear fragrance oil and stir well.

**7.** Portion the soap batter into the molds. In 20-24 hours take the soap out of the molds and cut it. Place the soap on the balcony for a week or two. Give the soap some time because the saponification process should end.

**During the soap preparation process always use rubber gloves, goggles, long sleeves and breathing mask.**

# Goat Milk, Grapefruit and Avocado Soap

**Prep Time: about 60 minutes**

**Cooking Time: 40 minutes**

## Ingredients:

- 10 oz grapefruit essential oil
- 2 tablespoons grapefruit zest, minced
- 2 avocados, diced
- 15 oz olive oil
- 14 oz palm oil
- 7 oz castor oil
- 1 tablespoon liquid Vitamin A
- 10-12 oz goat milk
- 9 oz 100% pure lye

## How to Make Homemade Soap:

**1.** Mash the avocado with the fork or potato masher.

**2.** Pour some water and blend well using the stick blender until there is a creamy mass.

**3.** Spoon the lye into the goat milk and mix well until there is a creamy consistency.

**4.** Combine the olive, palm and castor oils. Then melt them over the low heat for around 20 minutes.

**5.** Pour the lye and goat milk mixture into the oils and stir well.

**6.** Spoon the avocado puree and blend well.

**7.** Cook the lye, avocado and oils mixture over the low heat for about 20 minutes. Keep stirring to prevent the soap batter from rising.

**8.** Use a PH test to check if the soap is ready. Ideal values are between 7 and 10. If the indicator is higher than 10, then this means that the soap is not ready.

**9.** Add in the vitamin A, grapefruit essential oil and minced grapefruit zest. Blend all the ingredients well using a stick blender until there is a creamy mass.

**10.** Pour the soap batter into the molds. In 20-24 hours take the soap out of the molds and cut it into bars. Wait for two or three weeks and then start using the soap.


**During the soap preparation process always use rubber gloves, goggles, long sleeves and breathing mask.**

# Goat Milk, Orange and Banana Soap for Delicate Skin

**Prep Time: about 40-50 minutes**

**Cooking Time: 30 minutes**

## Ingredients:

- 15 oz orange essential oil
- 2 tablespoons orange zest, minced
- 1 banana
- 15 oz olive oil
- 14 oz palm oil
- 10 oz castor oil
- 1 tablespoon Vitamin D
- 1 tablespoon Vitamin A
- 10 oz goat milk
- 8-9 oz lye

## How to Make Homemade Soap:

**1.** Mash the banana.

**2.** Add the lye to the cold goat milk and mix well until the pureed mass.

**3.** Combine the olive, palm and castor oils. Then melt them over the low heat for 20 minutes.

**4.** Pour the lye and goat milk batter into the oils and stir well.

**5.** Spoon the banana puree and blend using a stick blender until there is a creamy and pureed mass.

**6.** Cook the lye, banana, orange zest and oils mixture over the low heat for about 20 minutes. Keep stirring to prevent the soap batter from burning and rising. Then set the soap batter aside to cool it.

**7.** Use a PH test to check if the soap is ready. Ideal values are between 7 and 10. If the indicator is higher than 10, then this means that the soap is not ready.

**8.** Spoon the orange essential oil, vitamin D and vitamin A. Stir the ingredients well.

**9.** Pour the soap batter into the molds. In 20-24 hours take the soap out of the molds and cut into pieces. Wait for few weeks and then start using the soap.


**During the soap preparation process always use rubber gloves, goggles, long sleeves and breathing mask.**

# Goat Milk, Grapefruit and Orange Soap

**Prep Time: about 60-70 minutes**

**Cooking Time: 60 minutes**

**Ingredients:**

- 15 oz grapefruit essential oil
- 10 oz folded orange essential oil
- 7 oz grapefruit zest, minced
- 16 oz olive oil
- 14 oz palm oil
- 10 oz castor oil
- 2 teaspoons Vitamin C
- 10 oz cold goat milk
- 8 oz lye

## How to Make Homemade Soap:

**1.** Pour the lye into the cold goat milk and mix well. Cool for around 30 minutes.

**2.** Melt the olive, palm and castor oils over the low heat for about 10-20 minutes.

**3.** Cool the oils and then pour the lye and goat milk mixture into the oils. Mix in the grapefruit zest and stir well.

**4.** Cook the lye and oils mixture over the low heat for about 40 minutes.

**5.** Use a PH test to check if the soap is ready. Ideal values are between 7 and 10. If the indicator is higher than 10, then this means that the soap is not ready.

**6.** Add in the grapefruit essential oil, orange essential oil and vitamin C. Blend the soap batter well.

**7.** Pour the soap batter into the molds. In 20-24 hours take the soap out of the molds and cut it into pieces. Wait for few weeks and then use your soap.

During the soap preparation process always use the rubber gloves, goggles, long sleeves and breathing mask.

# Goat Milk, Grapefruit and Orange and Green Tea Soap

**Prep Time: about 60-70 minutes**

**Cooking Time: 60 minutes**

## Ingredients:

- 15 oz grapefruit essential oil
- 10 oz folded orange essential oil
- 10 oz green tea essential oil
- 7 oz grapefruit zest, minced
- 16 oz olive oil
- 14 oz palm oil
- 10 oz castor oil
- 2 teaspoons Vitamin C
- 10 oz cold goat milk
- 8 oz lye

## How to Make Homemade Soap:

**1.** Pour the lye into the cold goat milk and mix well. Cool for around 30 minutes.

**2.** Melt the olive, palm and castor oils over the low heat for about 10-20 minutes.

**3.** Cool the oils and then pour the lye and goat milk mixture into the oils. Mix in the grapefruit zest and stir well.

**4.** Cook the lye and oils mixture over the low heat for about 40 minutes.

**5.** Use a PH test to check if the soap is ready. Ideal values are between 7 and 10. If the indicator is higher than 10, then this means that the soap is not ready.

**6.** Add in the green tea essential oil, grapefruit essential oil, orange essential oil and vitamin C.

**7.** Pour the soap batter into the molds. In 20-24 hours take the soap out of the molds and cut it into pieces. Wait for few weeks and then use your soap.

**During the soap preparation process always use the rubber gloves, goggles, long sleeves and breathing mask.**

# Goat Milk, Cherry, Orange and Apple Soap

**Prep Time: about 40-50 minutes**

**Cooking Time: 50 minutes**

## Ingredients:

- 12 oz cherry essential oil
- 10 oz apple fragrance oil
- 4 oz orange zest, minced
- 15 oz olive oil
- 14 oz palm oil
- 14 oz castor oil
- 7 oz shea butter
- 10 oz goat milk
- 8 oz 100% pure lye

## How to Make Homemade Soap:

**1.** Spoon the lye into the cold goat milk and mix well until the creamy mass.

**2.** Mix together the olive, palm and castor oils with the shea butter and melt the oils in the microwave for 20 minutes. Then stir the oils and shea butter well.

**3.** With the mask, rubber gloves and goggles pour the lye and goat milk batter into the oils and stir well.

**4.** Cook the lye and oils mixture over the low heat for about 30 minutes. Keep stirring to prevent the soap batter from burning and rising.

**5.** Use a PH test to check if the soap is ready. Ideal values are between 7 and 10. If the indicator is higher than 10, but lower than 7, then this means that the soap is not ready.

**6.** Add in the cherry essential oil and apple fragrance oil and stir well.

**7.** Portion the soap batter into the molds. In 20-24 hours take the soap out of the molds and cut it. Wait for a few weeks and only then use the soap.

**During the soap preparation process always use rubber gloves, goggles, long sleeves and breathing mask.**

# Goat Milk, Grapefruit and Lemon Soap with Lavender

**Prep Time: about 70-80 minutes**

**Cooking Time: 60 minutes**

**Ingredients:**

- 15 oz grapefruit essential oil
- 12 oz lemon essential oil
- 12 oz lavender essential oil
- 16 oz palm oil
- 14 oz olive oil
- 14 oz coconut oil
- 10 oz goat milk
- 8 oz pure lye

**How to Make Homemade Soap:**

**1.** Add the lye to the cold goat milk and mix well. Cool the lye and goat milk batter well.

**2.** In a pot, combine the palm, olive and coconut oils. Then melt the oils over the low heat for around 20 minutes.

**3.** Pour the lye and goat milk mixture into the oils and mix well.

**4.** Cook the lye and oils mixture over the low heat for about 40 minutes. Keep stirring to prevent the soap batter from burning and rising.

**5.** Use a PH test to check if the soap is ready. Ideal values are between 7 and 10. If the indicator is lower than 7 and higher than 10, then this means that the soap is not ready.

**6.** Spoon the grapefruit essential oil, lemon essential oil and lavender essential oil. Blend the mix using a stick blender.

**7.** Pour the soap batter into the molds. In 20-24 hours take the soap out of the molds. Cut the soap into pieces and wait for two or three weeks until the process of the saponification will complete and only then use the soap.

During the soap preparation process always use rubber gloves, goggles, long sleeves and breathing masks.

# Goat Milk, Grapefruit and Orange Soap with Honey

**Prep Time: about 60 minutes**

**Cooking Time: 50 minutes**

## Ingredients:

- 14 oz grapefruit essential oil
- 10 oz orange essential oil
- 3 tablespoons liquid honey
- 16 oz olive oil
- 16 oz castor oil
- 12 oz palm oil
- 2 teaspoons coconut butter
- 10 oz goat milk
- 8 oz lye

## How to Make Homemade Soap:

**1.** Spoon the lye into the goat milk and mix well.

**2.** In a pot, combine the coconut butter with the olive, castor and palm oils. Then melt the butter and oils over the low heat for around 20 minutes.

**3.** Pour the lye and goat milk batter into the oils and mix well.

**4.** Cook the lye and oils mixture over the low heat for about 30 minutes. Keep stirring to prevent the soap batter from burning and rising. Then set the soap batter aside to cool it.

**5.** Use a PH test to check if the soap is ready. Ideal values are between 7 and 10. If the indicator is higher than 10, then this means that the soap is not ready.

**6.** Mix in the orange essential oil, grapefruit essential oil and liquid honey. Blend all the ingredients using a stick blender.

**7.** Pour the grapefruit soap mixture into the molds. In 20-24 hours take the soap out of the molds. Wait for two weeks and use the soap.

During the soap preparation process always use rubber gloves, goggles, long sleeves and breathing mask.

# Goat Milk, Lemon, Orange and Cherry Soap

**Prep Time: about 40-50 minutes**

**Cooking Time: 50 minutes**

**Ingredients:**

- 10 oz lemon essential oil
- 10 oz orange essential oil
- 10 oz cherry essential oil
- 16 oz olive oil
- 14 oz palm oil
- 14 oz coconut oil
- 3 tablespoons shea butter
- 12 oz goat milk
- 9 oz lye

**How to Make Homemade Soap:**

**1.** Spoon the lye into the cold goat milk and mix well until there is a creamy and smooth mass. The fumes will be produced during this process, so wear the rubber gloves, goggles and breathing mask.

**2.** Combine the olive, palm and coconut oils with the shea butter and melt the oils for 20 minutes. Then stir the oils and shea butter well.

**3.** Use the mask, rubber gloves and goggles and ladle the lye and goat milk mixture into the oils and stir well.

**4.** Cook the lye and oils mixture over the low heat for about half and hour. Keep stirring to prevent the soap batter from burning and rising.

**5.** Use a PH test to check if the soap is ready. Ideal values are between 7 and 10. If the indicator is higher than 10, but lower than 7, then this means that the soap is not ready.

**6.** Spoon the grapefruit essential oil, orange essential oil and cherry essential oil and stir well.

**7.** Portion the soap batter into the molds. In 20-24 hours take the soap out of the molds and cut it. Wait for a few weeks and only then use the soap.

**During the soap preparation process always use rubber gloves, goggles, long sleeves and breathing mask.**

# Goat Milk, Cherry, Kiwi and Apple Soap

**Prep Time: about 40-50 minutes**

**Cooking Time: 50 minutes**

**Ingredients:**

- 12 oz cherry essential oil
- 10 oz apple fragrance oil
- 10 oz kiwi essential oil
- 15 oz olive oil
- 14 oz palm oil
- 14 oz castor oil
- 7 oz shea butter
- 10 oz goat milk
- 8 oz 100% pure lye

## How to Make Homemade Soap:

**1.** Spoon the lye into the cold goat milk and mix well until the creamy mass.

**2.** Mix together the olive, palm and castor oils with the shea butter and melt the oils in the microwave for 20 minutes. Then stir the oils and shea butter well.

**3.** With the mask, rubber gloves and goggles pour the lye and goat milk batter into the oils and stir well.

**4.** Cook the lye and oils mixture over the low heat for about 30 minutes. Keep stirring to prevent the soap batter from burning and rising.

**5.** Use a PH test to check if the soap is ready. Ideal values are between 7 and 10. If the indicator is higher than 10, but lower than 7, then this means that the soap is not ready.

**6.** Add in the cherry essential oil, kiwi essential oil and apple fragrance oil and stir well.

**7.** Portion the soap batter into the molds. In 20-24 hours take the soap out of the molds and cut it. Wait for a few weeks and only then use the soap.

**During the soap preparation process always use rubber gloves, goggles, long sleeves and breathing mask.**

# Goat Milk, Orange and Peach Soap

**Prep Time: 50 minutes**

**Cooking Time: 40 minutes**

## Ingredients:

- 10 tablespoons orange essential oil
- 6 tablespoons peach extract
- 16 oz olive oil
- 14 oz palm oil
- 10 oz castor oil
- 2 tablespoons coconut butter
- 9 oz goat milk
- 8 oz lye

## How to Make Homemade Soap:

**1.** Spoon the lye into the goat milk and mix well until there is a homogenous mass. The fumes will be produced during this process, so wear the rubber gloves, goggles and breathing mask.

**2.** Meanwhile, in a pot, combine the olive, palm and castor oils. Melt the oils on a burner for 10 minutes.

**3.** Spoon the coconut butter and cook with the oils over the low heat for about 10 minutes.

**4.** Pour the lye and milk mixture into the oils and stir well. Add in the peach extract.

**5.** Cook the lye, peach extract and oils over the low heat for about 40 minutes. Keep stirring to prevent the soap batter from burning and rising. Then set the soap batter aside to cool it.

**6.** Use a PH test to check if the soap is ready. Ideal values are between 7 and 10. If the indicator is lower than 7, but higher than 10, then this means that the soap is not ready.

**7.** Spoon the orange essential oil into the lye and oils mixture and blend the ingredients well using a stick blender.

**8.** Pour the soap batter into the molds. In 20-24 hours take the soap out of the molds and leave for a few weeks.

**During the soap preparation process always use rubber gloves, goggles, long sleeves and breathing mask.**

# Goat Milk, Pear and Orange and Green Tea Soap

**Prep Time: about 60-70 minutes**

**Cooking Time: 60 minutes**

**Ingredients:**

- 15 oz pear essential oil
- 10 oz folded orange essential oil
- 10 oz green tea essential oil
- 16 oz olive oil
- 14 oz palm oil
- 14 oz castor oil
- 2 teaspoons Vitamin C
- 10 oz cold goat milk
- 8 oz lye

## How to Make Homemade Soap:

**1.** Pour the lye into the cold goat milk and mix well. Cool for around 30 minutes.

**2.** Melt the olive, palm and castor oils over the low heat for about 10-20 minutes.

**3.** Cool the oils and then pour the lye and goat milk mixture into the oils. Mix in the grapefruit zest and stir well.

**4.** Cook the lye and oils mixture over the low heat for about 40 minutes.

**5.** Use a PH test to check if the soap is ready. Ideal values are between 7 and 10. If the indicator is higher than 10, then this means that the soap is not ready.

**6.** Add in the green tea essential oil, pear essential oil, orange essential oil and vitamin C.

**7.** Pour the soap batter into the molds. In 20-24 hours take the soap out of the molds and cut it into pieces. Wait for few weeks and then use your soap.

During the soap preparation process always use the rubber gloves, goggles, long sleeves and breathing mask.

# Goat Milk, Lemon, Cherry and Almond Soap for Delicate Skin

**Prep Time: 65-75 minutes**

**Cooking Time: about 60 minutes**

**Ingredients:**

- 12 oz lemon essential oil
- 10 oz cherry fragrance oil
- 10 oz almond oil
- 14 oz olive oil
- 14 oz palm oil
- 12 oz castor oil
- 2 tablespoons vitamin D
- 10 oz cold goat milk
- 8 oz lye

**How to Make Homemade Soap:**

**1.** Add the lye to the goat milk and mix well until there is a smooth mass.

**2.** Combine the almond oil with the olive, palm and castor oils and melt them in a pot over the low heat for 20 minutes.

**3.** Pour the lye and goat milk mixture into the oils and mix well.

**4.** Boil the lye and oils mixture over the low heat for about 40 minutes. Keep stirring to prevent the soap batter from rising. Cool the soap batter.

**5.** Use a PH test to check if the soap is ready. Ideal values are between 7 and 10. If the indicator is higher than 10, then this means that the soap is not ready.

**6.** Mix in the lemon essential oil, cherry fragrance oil and vitamin D and stir the mixture well.

**7.** Spoon the soap batter into the molds. In 20-24 hours take the soap out of the molds and cut it into bars. Then wait for two or three weeks until the process of the saponification will complete and only then use the soap.

**During the soap preparation process always use rubber gloves, goggles, long sleeves and breathing mask.**

# Goat Milk, Lemon, Cherry and Coconut Soap

**Prep Time: about 80-90 minutes**

**Cooking Time: about 70-80 minutes**

**Ingredients:**

- 14 oz lemon essential oil
- 2 tablespoons lemon zest, minced
- 1 cup of fresh cherries, pitted
- 18 oz coconut oil
- 15 oz olive oil
- 10 oz castor oil
- 2 tablespoons shredded coconut
- 10 oz goat milk
- 8 oz lye

**How to Make Homemade Soap:**

**1.** In a pot, cook the cherries over the low heat for about 20 minutes and skim the foam. Then blend the cherries.

**2.** Slowly pour the lye into the cold goat milk and let it cool for around half an hour.

**3.** Combine the coconut oil with the olive and castor oils. Boil the oils on the burner for around 15 minutes.

**4.** Pour the lye and goat milk mixture into the oils. Add in the lemon zest and mix well.

**5.** Boil the lye/oils mixture with the cherries over the medium heat for about 40 minutes. Skim the foam.

**6.** Use a PH test to check if the soap is ready. Ideal values are between 7 and 10. If the indicator is lower than 7, but higher than 10, then the soap is not ready.

**7.** Mix in the lemon essential oil and shredded coconut and only then whisk well.

**8.** Pour the soap batter into the molds. In 20-24 hours take the soap out of the molds and cut it. Wait for two or three weeks until the process of the saponification will complete and then use the soap.

**During the soap preparation process always use rubber gloves, goggles, long sleeves and breathing mask.**

# Goat Milk, Grapefruit and Blueberry Soap

**Prep Time: about 80 minutes**

**Cooking Time: 70 minutes**

## Ingredients:

- 14 oz grapefruit fragrant oil
- 3 oz grapefruit zest, minced
- 1 cup of fresh blueberries
- 19 oz olive oil
- 15 oz palm oil
- 14 oz castor oil
- 7 oz shea butter
- 2 drops blue soap colorant
- 10 oz cold goat milk
- 8 oz lye

## How to Make Homemade Soap:

**1.** In a bowl, mash the blueberries. Then ladle the blueberries into the pot and boil them over the low heat for about 20 minutes. Skim the foam. Keep stirring to prevent the blueberries from burning.

**2.** Add the lye to the cold goat milk and mix well.

**3.** Mix together the olive, palm and castor oils. Then spoon the shea butter and melt the oils and butter over the low heat for 20 minutes.

**4.** Add the lye and goat milk batter to the oils and stir well.

**5.** Mix in the blue soap colorant and grapefruit zest into the lye and oils mixture and blend.

**6.** Melt the lye and oils mixture over the medium heat for about 30 minutes. Keep stirring to prevent the soap batter from burning and rising.

**7.** Use a PH test to check if the soap is ready. Ideal values are between 7 and 10.

**8.** Slowly pour the blueberries and grapefruit fragrant oil and blend them.

**9.** Pour the soap batter into the molds. After one or two days take the soap out of the molds. Leave the soap for 10 days and then use it. The soap needs some time because the saponification process should end.

**During the soap preparation process wear rubber gloves, goggles, long sleeves and breathing mask.**

# Goat Milk, Orange, Mango and Cinnamon Soap

**Prep Time: about 2 hours**

**Cooking Time: 55 minutes**

## Ingredients:

- 14 oz orange essential oil
- 10 oz mango essential oil
- 8 oz cinnamon essential oil
- 17 oz olive oil
- 12 oz palm oil
- 12 oz castor oil
- 4 oz cocoa butter
- 10 oz goat milk
- 8 oz lye

## How to Make Homemade Soap:

**1.** Pour the lye into the goat milk and mix well until there is a smooth mass. Then cool the lye.

**2.** In a pot, combine the olive oil, palm oil and castor oil. Add the cocoa butter and melt the mixture over the low heat for about 20 minutes.

**3.** Ladle the lye into the oils and blend using a stick blender until there is a homogenous mass.

**4.** Boil over the low heat for about 40 minutes. Keep stirring to prevent the soap batter from burning and rising. Then cool the soap batter.

**5.** Use a PH test to check if the soap is ready. Ideal values are between 7 and 10. If the indicator is lower than 7 and higher than 10, then the soap is not ready.

**6.** Add the orange essential oil, mango essential oil and cinnamon essential oil. Blend using a stick blender.

**7.** Ladle the soap batter into the molds. In 20-24 hours take the soap out of the molds and cut it into pieces. Then wait for two weeks.

# Goat Milk, Lemon, Green Tea and Lavender Soap

**Prep Time: about 45-50 minutes**

**Cooking Time: 40 minutes**

## Ingredients:

- 15 oz lemon essential oil
- 12 oz green tea oil
- 12 oz lavender essential oil
- 16 oz olive oil
- 16 oz palm oil
- 15 oz castor oil
- 3 oz coconut butter
- 3 oz shea butter
- 10 oz goat milk
- 8 oz 100% pure lye

## How to Make Homemade Soap:

**1.** Spoon the lye into the goat milk and mix well until there is a creamy mass. The fumes will be produced during this process. Then cool the mixture.

**2.** In a pot, combine the coconut butter, shea butter, olive, palm and castor oils. Melt the butter and oils on a burner for around 10 minutes.

**3.** Pour the lye into the oils mixture and mix well.

**4.** Boil the lye and oils mixture over the low heat for about 30 minutes and then set the soap batter to cool.

**5.** Use a PH test to check if the soap is ready. Ideal values are between 7 and 10.

**6.** Add in the lemon essential oil, green tea oil and lavender essential oil. Blend all the ingredients well.

**7.** Pour the soap batter into the molds. In 20-24 hours take the soap out of the molds and cut it into pieces. Wait two or three weeks and you are free to use the soap.

During the soap preparation process always use rubber gloves, goggles, long sleeves and breathing mask.

# Goat Milk, Mango, Lemon and Pear Soap

**Prep Time: about 90 minutes**

**Cooking Time: 80-90 minutes**

## Ingredients:

- 15 oz mango essential oil
- 12 oz lemon zest, minced
- 10 oz pear extract
- 2 medium pears, diced
- 15 oz coconut oil
- 14 oz palm oil
- 12 oz castor oil
- 4 oz shea butter
- 10 drops lemon essential oil
- 10 oz goat milk
- 8 oz lye

## How to Make Homemade Soap:

**1.** Preheat the oven to 300-320 degrees Fahrenheit. Grease the baking pan with some coconut oil. Spoon the diced pears into the baking pan and pour some water. Bake the pears for about 30 minutes and then mash them.

**2.** Spoon the lye into the cold goat milk and mix well until there is a smooth mass. The fumes will be produced during the process, so wear the rubber gloves, goggles and breathing mask. Let it cool for around 30 minutes.

**3.** Melt the coconut, palm and castor oils for 10 minutes.

**4.** Mix in the shea butter and melt with the oils over the low heat for around 20 minutes.

**5.** Put on a mask, rubber gloves and goggles. Add the lye and goat milk mixture to the oils and stir well.

**6.** Pour the pears puree into the lye and oils mixture. Add the lemon zest and blend using a stick blender until there is a pureed consistency.

**7.** Cook the lye, pears and oils soap batter over the low heat for about 30 minutes. Keep stirring to prevent the pears soap batter from burning. Set the soap batter aside to cool.

**8.** Use a PH test to check if the soap is ready. Ideal values are between 7 and 10. If the indicator is higher than 10, then this means that the soap is not ready.

**9.** Add the lemon essential oil, mango essential oil and pear extract into the lye, pears and oils mixture. Blend well.

**10.** Pour the soap batter into the silicon molds. In 20-24 hours take your soap out of the molds and cool it for a week or two. After week or two you are free to start using the soap.

**During the soap preparation process always use rubber gloves, goggles, long sleeves and breathing mask.**

# Goat Milk, Orange, Cherry, Pineapple and Cinnamon Soap

**Prep Time: about 90-95 minutes**

**Cooking Time: 80-85 minutes**

## Ingredients:

- 15 oz orange essential oil
- 2 teaspoons orange zest, minced
- 14 oz cherry essential oil
- 1 cup of pineapples, peeled and diced
- 12 oz pineapple fragrance oil
- 17 oz olive oil
- 13 oz palm oil
- 10 oz castor oil
- 4 teaspoons shea butter
- 2 tablespoons cinnamon essential oil
- 12 oz goat milk
- 9 oz lye

## How to Make Homemade Soap:

**1.** Spoon the diced pineapples into the pot. Pour some water and cook for about 20 minutes.

**2.** Open the oven and set the pineapples aside to cool until the temperature reaches around 80-90 degrees Fahrenheit.

**3.** Mash the pineapples using the potato masher until the pureed consistency.

**4.** Spoon the lye into the cold goat milk and mix well until there is a homogenous mass.

**5.** Mix together the olive oil, palm oil and castor oil. Then spoon the shea butter and melt the oils over the low heat for around 20 minutes.

**6.** Pour the lye and goat milk mixture into the oils and stir well.

**7.** Spoon the pineapple puree into the lye and oils mixture and blend using a stick blender until there is a creamy consistency. Mix in the orange zest.

**8.** Cook the lye, pineapple and oils mixture over the low heat for about 40 minutes. Keep stirring to prevent the apple soap batter from burning and rising. Then set the soap batter aside to cool it.

**9.** Use a PH test to check if the soap is ready. Ideal values are between 7 and 10. If the indicator is higher than 10, then this means that the soap is not ready.

**10.** Pour the cherry essential oil, orange essential oil, cinnamon essential oil and pineapple fragrance oil.

**11.** Pour the soap batter into the molds. In 20-24 hours take your soap out of the molds and cut it into the pieces. Then wait for two or three weeks and start using the soap.

**During the soap preparation process always use rubber gloves, goggles, long sleeves and breathing mask.**

# Goat Milk, Orange, Apple and Lavender Soap

**Prep Time: about 45-50 minutes**

**Cooking Time: 40 minutes**

**Ingredients:**

- 15 oz orange essential oil
- 14 oz apple essential oil
- 10 oz lavender essential oil
- 15 oz olive oil
- 15 oz palm oil
- 10 oz castor oil
- 6 oz shea butter
- 12 oz goat milk
- 10 oz lye

**How to Make Homemade Soap:**

**1.** Spoon the lye into the cold goat milk and mix well until there is a creamy consistency. The fumes will be produced during this process.

**2.** Melt the shea butter, olive, palm and castor oils over the low heat for about 10 minutes.

**3.** Pour the lye and goat milk mixture into the oils and mix well.

**4.** Boil the lye and oils mixture over the low heat for about 30 minutes and then set the soap batter to cool.

**5.** Use a PH test to check if the soap is ready. Ideal values are between 7 and 10.

**6.** Mix in the orange essential oil, apple essential oil and lavender essential oil. Blend well.

**7.** Pour the soap batter into the molds. In 20-24 hours take the soap out of the molds and cut it into pieces. Wait two or three weeks and you are free to use the soap.

During the soap preparation process always use rubber gloves, goggles, long sleeves and breathing mask.

# Goat Milk, Orange and Blueberry Soap

**Prep Time: about 80 minutes**

**Cooking Time: 70 minutes**

## Ingredients:

- 15 oz orange essential oil
- 7 oz orange zest, minced
- 1 cup of fresh blueberries
- 16 oz olive oil
- 12 oz coconut oil
- 12 oz castor oil
- 7 oz shea butter
- 2 drops blue soap colorant
- 12 oz goat milk
- 10 oz lye

## How to Make Homemade Soap:

**1.** In a bowl, mash the blueberries. Then ladle the blueberries into a pot and boil them over the low heat for about 20 minutes. Skim the foam.
**2.** Add the lye to the goat milk and mix well.
**3.** Mix together the olive, coconut and castor oils. Then spoon the shea butter and melt the oils and butter over the low heat for 20 minutes.
**4.** Add the lye and goat milk mixture to the oils and stir well.
**5.** Mix in the blueberries, blue soap colorant and orange zest into the lye and oils mixture and blend using a stick blender until the pureed consistency.
**6.** Melt the mixture over the medium heat for about 30 minutes. Keep stirring to prevent the soap batter from burning and rising.
**7.** Use a PH test to check if the soap is ready. Ideal values are between 7 and 10.
**8.** Add in the orange essential oil. Blend the ingredients well.

**9.** Pour the soap batter into the molds. After one or two days take the soap out of the molds.

**During the soap preparation process wear rubber gloves, goggles, long sleeves and breathing mask.**

# Goat Milk, Kiwi, Pineapple, Cherry and Coconut Soap

**Prep Time: about 80-90 minutes**

**Cooking Time: about 70-80 minutes**

## Ingredients:

- 14 oz kiwi essential oil
- 12 oz pineapple essential oil
- 2 tablespoons lemon zest, minced
- 1 cup of fresh cherries, pitted
- 18 oz coconut oil
- 15 oz olive oil
- 10 oz castor oil
- 2 tablespoons shredded coconut
- 12 oz goat milk
- 9 oz lye

## How to Make Homemade Soap:

**1.** In a pot, cook the cherries over the low heat for about 20 minutes and skim the foam. Then blend the cherries.

**2.** Pour the lye into the cold goat milk and let it cool for around 30 minutes.

**3.** Mix together the coconut oil with the olive and castor oils. Boil the oils on the burner for around 15 minutes.

**4.** Pour the lye and goat milk mixture into the oils. Add in the lemon zest and mix well.

**5.** Boil the lye/oils mixture with the cherries over the medium heat for about 40 minutes.

**6.** Use a PH test to check if the soap is ready. Ideal values are between 7 and 10. If the indicator is lower than 7, but higher than 10, then the soap is not ready.

**7.** Mix in the kiwi essential oil and pineapple essential oil. Then pour the shredded coconut and only then whisk well.

**8.** Pour the soap batter into the molds. In 20-24 hours take the soap out of the molds and cut it. Wait for two or three weeks until the process of the saponification will complete and then use the soap.

**During the soap preparation process always use rubber gloves, goggles, long sleeves and breathing mask.**

# Conclusion

Thank you for buying this goat milk soap book. I hope this book was helpful in preparing natural goat milk soaps.

If you are new in this field, this book will help you start your soap journey. The recipes in this book are simple, and the process of preparing homemade soaps is explained in the simple way. Those you can use, when the level of experience will grow and you will feel more confident. But never give up, always be open to learn and try new soap recipes.

Thank you again and I hope you have enjoyed this soap cooking book.

Made in the USA
Las Vegas, NV
23 October 2023

79600976R00057